LEEDS

A Photographic Journey
Through Yorkshire's Largest City

PHOTOGRAPHS: TONY QUINN

TEXT: MELVYN JONES

MYRIAD
LONDON

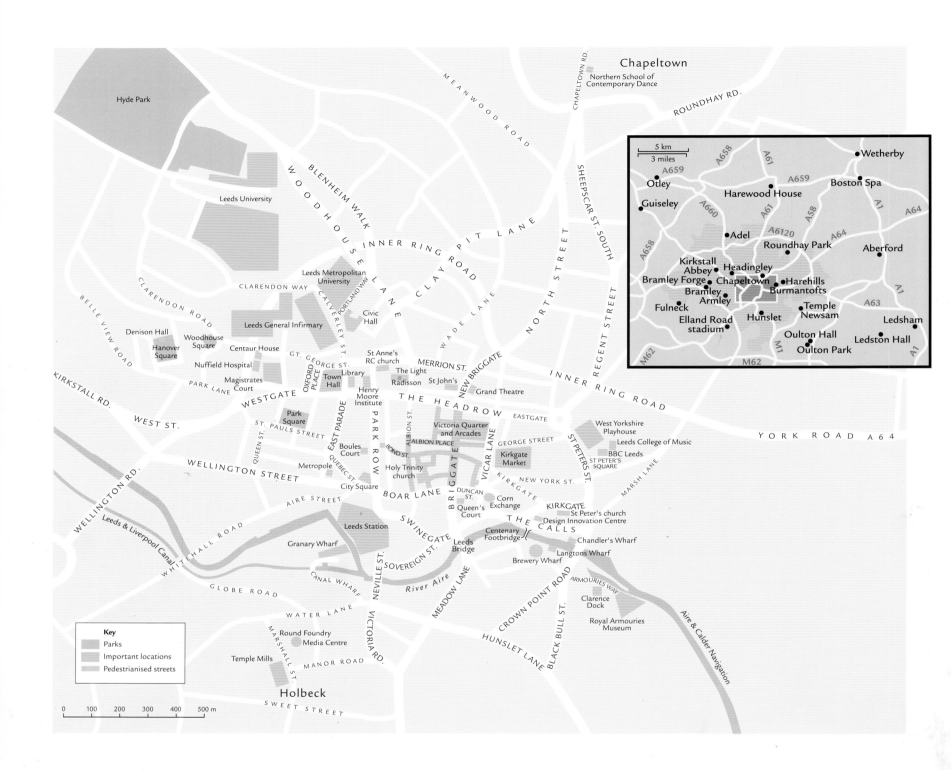

First published in 2008 by Myriad Books Limited
35 Bishopsthorpe Road, London SE26 4PA

Photographs copyright © Tony Quinn
Text copyright © Melvyn Jones

ISBN 1 84746 136 0
EAN 978 1 84746 136 0

Designed by Jerry Goldie Graphic Design
Printed in China

www.myriadbooks.com

CONTENTS

INTRODUCTION

Leeds, as *Loidis*, was first mentioned, by the Venerable Bede, in the early eighth century. It was given borough status by the lord of the manor, Maurice Paynel, in 1207. It thrived as a market town for hundreds of years, the original cloth market being held on Leeds Bridge. Daniel Defoe, in the 1720s, described the town as being "wealthy and populous" and said that its cloth market was "not to be equalled in the world".

It was the development of water and rail transport that transformed Leeds into an industrial giant. In 1699 an Act was passed to create the Aire and Calder Navigation and in 1816 the Leeds and Liverpool Canal was completed. The first railway was the Leeds to Selby railway which was opened in 1834 (linking the town to Hull), and in 1842 the Midland railway to London was opened, closely followed by the Leeds and Bradford railway and the Manchester and Leeds railway.

Leeds became not only an important woollen cloth manufacturing centre but also a centre for the production of linen, earthenware and a wide variety of engineering products including textile machinery. Today it is well-served by motorways (M1, M62 and A1M) and Leeds Bradford Airport.

It is the commercial and financial metropolis of Yorkshire with important government offices, the headquarters of Yorkshire Television, BBC Yorkshire region, and of Yorkshire's regional newspaper, the *Yorkshire Post*, two large universities and a flourishing retail sector, with shops to suit every taste, in some unusual and historically important locations.

Reflecting its medieval origins, its prosperous industrial past, and its present important regional, commercial, financial and educational role, the city of Leeds is full of interesting buildings and spaces. Besides a wide range of modern architecture it contains medieval churches, the remains of a medieval abbey, a scattering of grand country houses built between the 17th and 19th centuries, the villas of prosperous Victorian manufacturers, grand public buildings, factories and warehouses now converted to other uses, Britain's largest indoor market and some remarkable covered shopping arcades. And these buildings and spaces are not all concentrated in the central urban area but also along the revived Waterfront, in the suburbs and in the outlying towns and villages.

So turn the page and begin your guided tour...

PART ONE

THE CITY CENTRE

Leeds' compact city centre stretches from the City Station and City Square in the south, to Millennium Square and the Civic Hall in the north and from the Inner Ring Road in the west to Quarry Hill in the east. Within this area is a trellis of medieval streets and courts or yards, still carrying medieval names such as Briggate, Kirkgate and Swinegate (gate being from the Old Norse *gata* meaning a lane not a gate). Despite 19th and 20th century changes and insertions these early streets and yards still form the basic street network of the area. Within this central area there is a glorious mix of interesting buildings of every age, shape and size. There are churches, from the 17th to the 20th century, public buildings such as the Town Hall, Civic Hall and municipal buildings reflecting Leeds' rise and rise as a major town and then city, and architectural gems such as the General Infirmary, the Corn Exchange, the Grand Theatre, the Hotel Metropole and Whitelock's Pub. But above all there is the cathedral-like City Market Hall and County, Cross, Grand, Queen's and Thornton's shopping arcades, the City Market being the largest covered market in the country and the arcades being among the earliest examples of up-market covered shopping areas.

Leeds Bridge

The old medieval bridge is said to have been constructed from stones removed from the castle which had been built in 1169 but demolished in the 13th century. The old bridge had been a replacement for a ferry and ford across the river Aire. It was the main entry into the town from the south, leading directly to the main street of the medieval town, Briggate. The old bridge was widened twice in the 18th century before a completely new bridge replaced it. This Victorian bridge, which survives to this day, was built between 1870 and 1873. It has a single arch of cast-iron surmounted by a cast-iron balustrade of linked rings decorated by flower heads from John Butler's Ironworks in Stanningley. The city's coat of arms, displayed prominently on Leeds Bridge (right), dates back to the 1660s and contains three stars from the coat of arms of the first mayor, Thomas Danby, owls from the coat of arms of the first alderman, Sir John Savile and a fleece, the sign of the wool stapler, reflecting the wool industry's important role in Leeds' history.

River Aire

Leeds' principal river flows for 68 miles (110 km) from near Malham in the Pennines to its confluence with the river Ouse near Goole. At Leeds it was fordable, making the northern bank a good settlement site. The ford was then supplemented by a ferry and finally both were supplanted by Leeds Bridge. The exact origin of its name is a matter of debate – one authority suggests that it comes from the Old Celtic, meaning "strong river"; another suggests that it is from the Old English word *eg* meaning "an island, land partly surrounded by water" adapted by Old Norse speakers into *eyjar*, meaning islands, which is taken to refer to the braided nature of the river's course in its lower reaches.

Whitelock's

Standing in the narrow Turk's Yard at the top of Briggate is Whitelock's Pub or, as it was named in the 1880s by the then landlord John Upton Whitelock, "Whitelock's First City Luncheon Bar". There has been a public house here since at least the early 18th century, then the Turk's Head Inn. The interior of Whitelock's Pub is very richly decorated with stained glass, engraved mirrors, marble counters, faience tiles and shiny brasswork. Having a quiet drink here, the visitor can almost believe time has stopped in a bygone age.

Briggate shopping

Briggate (an Old Norse name simply meaning Bridge Street) was laid out in 1207 and from the outset was at the centre of Leeds' commercial quarter, housing at one time the cloth market and the annual fair. Pedestrianised north of Boar Lane it is still a magnet for shoppers and contains the stores of two Leeds institutions, Marks & Spencer (under the clock above) and Burton's tailoring. Michael Marks, one of the founders of M&S, started his business with a penny stall in Leeds Market in 1884. Montague Burton began his tailoring business in 1900. One of the origins of the expression "The Full Monty" is thought to be a three-piece wedding suit bought or hired from Burton's.

Holy Trinity

Holy Trinity church is just off Briggate on Boar Lane. This early 18th century church (built between 1722-27) by William Etty of York is in the Classical style. The exterior is constructed from locally quarried millstone grit and on the south side facing Boar Lane there are two doors and five round-headed windows separated by tall Doric pilasters (right). The present 188ft (55m) tower is a replacement, the original one having been blown down in a storm in 1839. Impressed into the lead drainpipes are fleeces (sheep hanging from a ring) that remind the modern visitor of the important role of woollen clothmaking in the history of Leeds. The interior is light and airy, with the nave flanked by tall Corinthian columns. At the east end is an early Victorian stained-glass window portraying the Ascension. Major restoration was carried out in the 1880s and the crammed box pews, galleries and choir stalls were removed.

Briggate

When Briggate (below) was laid out in the early 13th century, stretching northwards from Leeds Bridge to the Headrow, the areas behind the street front were almost as important as the street itself. Thirty building plots were allocated in the original deed. These areas of land could be divided up (which many were), bought or sold. They multiplied in number and became a series of long, narrow building plots, called "burgage" plots, because they were occupied by the citizens (burgesses) of the town. Their shape reflects the desire of shop, workshop and other workplace owners to have a commercial frontage on the main street.

Queen's Court

Over time, behind the street frontage of Briggate in the narrow plots, usually reached by a covered passage or "ginnel", the narrow yards or courts were filled with small cottages, workshops, inns and taverns. Queen's Court (left) is a case in point. At the front, at street level, is an eight-bayed house, originally built for a wool cloth merchant in c1714 that had workshops and warehouses behind, reached through a narrow covered passage. An alley still survives out of the back of the court into Calls Lane.

Duncan Street

Boar Lane bisects Briggate on the west, and Duncan Street bisects it on the east. The north side of Duncan Street was rebuilt about 1900, but the south side has late Victorian and 20th century buildings. The shops and offices along Duncan Street are built in a variety of styles including Jacobean, Baroque revival and Art Deco and use a variety of materials including terracotta and faience from the Burmantofts works of the Leeds Fireclay Company. The "bendy bus" is a modern phenomenon!

Briggate

Briggate lies at the hub of Leeds' modern retailing quarter, forming the spine leading from Leeds Bridge to the Headrow, with off-shoots along Boar Lane, Duncan Street and Kirkgate. This very wide street is lined with nationally known department stores and shops as well as independent retailers. Besides the shops fronting Briggate itself, running off Briggate at its northern end are the Thornton's Arcade, Queen's Arcade, and, in the Victoria Quarter, County Arcade and Cross Arcade, four of the five Victorian and Edwardian covered shopping arcades for which Leeds is famous. Now largely pedestrianised, Briggate attracts shoppers not only from all parts of Leeds, but also from the rest of West Yorkshire and beyond by car, bus and train. On a typical shopping day (which now, except for Christmas Day, extends for seven days a week and most days until mid-evening) the street and its shops are crowded with shoppers. On busy days, with street traders and street musicians, Briggate almost takes on its medieval character when the cloth market and annual fair took place there – without the smells, thank goodness!

Harvey Nichols & Dysons

Harvey Nichols' first department store outside London opened on the edge of the Victoria Quarter on the east side of Briggate in 1997. The main entrance to the store in Briggate is striking - glazed from ground floor to roof level, inserted between traditional Leeds frontages in brick. The uniformed doorman adds a metropolitan flavour to Briggate.

At the lower end of Briggate the most curious set of buildings are the Time Ball Buildings of John Dyson & Sons, jewellers, who began business in 1865 and closed in 1990. The buildings take their name from the time ball above the main clock outside the shop (left). The time ball clock, which was put up in 1910, was originally linked to Greenwich and the ball dropped at precisely 1pm each day. A second clock on the building (on the far left in the photograph) has a carved figure of Old Father Time over the top.

Queen's Arcade

The treasures of the retail quarter are the covered shopping arcades: Thornton's Arcade (1877-8), Grand Arcade (1897), Queen's Arcade (1899) and the County and Cross Arcades (1898-1904) of the Victoria Quarter. The arcades were a revolution. For the first time shoppers could be dry and warm in the worst of weathers. They were built along the long narrow burgage plots that had survived from the medieval town. The Queen's Arcade (above and right) was built on what had been the Rose & Crown Yard that extended for about 70 yards between Briggate and Lands Lane. The arcade is two-storeyed with originally the Queen's Arcade Hotel along the north side. It was restored in 1991-92.

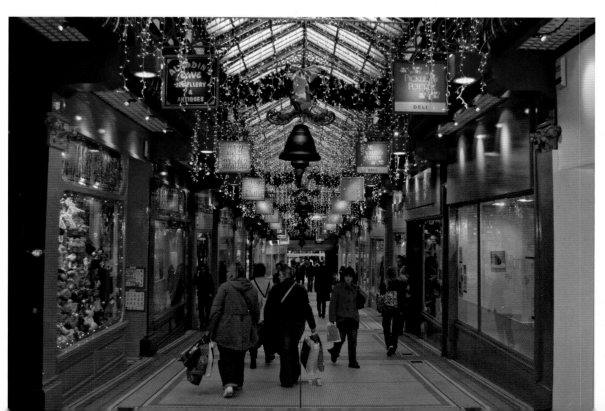

Thornton's Arcade

Thornton's was the first of Leeds' covered shopping arcades, built over the Old Talbot Inn Yard by Charles Thornton, brewer, victualler and owner of the Varieties Music Hall, which he had built on the site of a public house in 1865. The arcade, which was restored between 1990-92, is in the Gothic style. An attractive feature of Thornton's Arcade is the large clock (right) made by local clockmaker William Potts. Beneath the clock a group of characters from Sir Walter Scott's *Ivanhoe* – Richard Coeur de Lion, Robin Hood, Friar Tuck and Gurth the swineherd – strike the bell to announce the time.

County Arcade

The County Arcade, which with Cross Arcade and the recently covered Queen Victoria Street constitute the Victoria Quarter, presents the visitor with one of the most beautiful shopping environments in the city. There are shops selling clothing, lingerie, shoes and accessories, jewellery and beauty products. The arcade is 394ft (120m) long and has mahogany shopfronts with curved glass windows, separated by pilasters and columns of Siena marble above which are balustraded balconies crowned by an arched cast-iron roof. There are three glazed domes which give the arcade a feeling of space and light. Immediately under the central dome are mosaics depicting crafts and industries for which Leeds was once famous. The iron balconies are mainly painted green with a white Yorkshire rose motif. Above the archways at balcony level are bunches of oranges against a green foliage background. As part of the 1988-90 restoration the floors were re-laid and there is a particularly splendid circular mosaic design beneath the central dome.

Arcade architecture

The architecture and decorative detail of Leeds' covered shopping arcades reflect the late Victorian and early Edwardian period when they were built, a period when much re-building and re-design of central Leeds was taking place. The use of patterned and pierced cast iron for the arched roof-trusses is universal, allowing great strength to be allied with maximum light penetration. The employment of cast iron also reflects the use made of local firms in constructing the new arcades.

Decorative work

Local firms were also used in the decoration of the arcades. Note has already been made of the use of William Potts, the clockmaker, to provide an unusual clock for Thornton's Arcade. Another one is found in the Grand Arcade in New Briggate, this time with knights in armour guarding a castle whose doors swing open to reveal other figures in medieval costume. Full use was also made of terracotta decorative bricks and tiles and faience from the Burmantofts Works of Leeds Firebrick Company for decoration.

Victoria Quarter

The present-day Victoria Quarter, between Briggate and Vicar Lane, was created in 1989-90 by the roofing over of Queen Victoria Street (below) thus connecting County Arcade and Cross Arcade. The roof of the former Queen Victoria Street is made of blue, green, red and yellow glass in an abstract design. The street itself now has a tiled floor, seating areas, cafes, fountains and foliage. Many of the shops have mahogany woodwork and polished granite fronts and, besides Harvey Nichols, are home to more than two dozen of the country's leading designer brands. The Victoria Quarter as a whole has been nicknamed "the Knightsbridge of the North". On a more serious note the Victoria Quarter has recently been awarded a Gold Standard from the Tidy Business Awards Scheme for reducing, re-using and recycling waste rather than sending large amounts to landfill.

St John's, New Briggate

St John the Evangelist's church (above and right) was consecrated in 1634. It was the gift of John Harrison, a wealthy woollen cloth merchant. By the 1860s it was thought so dark and decrepit that demolition was planned. But the building attracted the support of architects Richard Norman Shaw and Sir George Gilbert Scott and restoration replaced the proposed demolition. Shaw oversaw the restoration in the 1860s and further work took place in the 1880s to undo some of the earlier restoration. The interior houses two naves side by side, interesting timber roof trusses and fine 17th century carved woodwork.

City Markets

The two panoramic views of central Leeds shown here of the City Market (right) and City Square (below) are among the most familiar city sights to residents and visitors alike. The market hall, at the junction of Kirkgate and Vicar Lane, was built in 1904 by architects John and Joseph Leeming, replacing the original market hall of 1857. A disastrous fire in 1975 destroyed two-thirds of the interior and another fire in 1992 set back restoration work that had begun in 1991. Now the exterior stonework has been repaired, the domes rebuilt and shop units and stalls replaced or repaired in their original style. Other surrounding Victorian market buildings have been restored and the open market has been provided with new stalls and a central market square created. The City Market is the largest covered market in the country with a large number of traders operating under its roof.

City Square

Old and new buildings jostle beside each other in City Square, the first city-scape seen by visitors arriving by train at the City Station. This space was created in the decade between 1893 and 1903 to celebrate the elevation of the town of Leeds to city status. The new square was the idea of T Walter Harding, textile engineer, who was mayor of Leeds in 1899 and who in the same decade was responsible for the building of another Leeds landmark, the Tower Works, on Globe Road beside the Leeds and Liverpool Canal. The square was redesigned in 2002 by the civic architect, John Thorp, when the fountains were installed. Dominating the view on the left is the old General Post Office (now closed as a post office and used in part for new cafes and restaurants) built in 1896. In front of the post office building are four statues, representing James Watt, John Harrison, Dean Hook and Joseph Priestley.

No 1 City Square

Standing next to the old General Post Office, but in complete contrast to it both in terms of architectural style and building materials, is No1 City Square, completed in 1998 to replace a 1960s block on the same site that was demolished in 1995. This 12-storey block has a black granite base, white limestone upper storeys and external liftshaft. Projecting from the top of the building over the glazed sections is a large sunshade. The offices within No 1 City Square are all set around a central atrium.

Leeds City Markets

Matching the grandeur of the exterior of the Leeds City Markets building is the majesty of the interior structure and architectural detail. If the exterior looks like a cathedral, then the inside looks like a giant circus big top. The cast-iron framework has not only allowed it to be structurally sound but also light and spacious. The detail on the ironwork has been picked out in various colours. Decorations include two Leeds coats of arms (above) and the photograph (centre) shows one of the many red scaly dragons with its tail entwined round an elaborately designed bracket.

The architecture of the City Markets is matched by the energy and bustle generated by the traders and their customers. The stalls, more like small shops than mere stalls, are separated by a network of paved walkways. Everything can be bought here from fresh fruit and vegetables, meat, confectionary, sweets and chocolates (from the "Toffee King"), to greetings cards, shoes, clothes, handbags and jewellery. You can even get your hair cut and your nails painted. And the crowded counter displays are attractive and appealing.

St Peter's Church

St Peter's, Leeds parish church, standing in Kirkgate ("lane to the church") was built between 1837-41, to replace the medieval church at a cost of £30,000. It was denied cathedral status in the late 19th century. Its tall, far from plain tower topped by battlements and pinnacles, is a Leeds landmark. Unlike most parish churches, St Peter's stands not in a central position, but in a rather peripheral one, compared with St John's, and St Anne's the Roman Catholic cathedral. This outer location was emphasised by the building of the railway embankment to the north in the 19th century but this is now counter-balanced by the redevelopment of the Waterfront to the south.

The interior of the church (below), which was restored in 1989, is large and contains some interesting furnishings. By the south door stands a 15th century octagonal font with a 17th century cover and near the altar there is an Anglo-Saxon cross. There are also many important monuments including one to Ralph Thoresby, the antiquary, who was born in Kirkgate and who died in 1725. Thoresby wrote the first history of Leeds and his name is commemorated in the name of the Leeds and District historical society, the Thoresby Society, founded in 1889. The oldest monument in the church is of a knight of the early 14th century (left), lying with his hands together and his legs crossed.

Corn Exchange

The Corn Exchange, like the Town Hall, is the work of the Hull-born architect Cuthbert Brodrick, who won first prize for his design in a stiff competition. The building is in the shape of an ellipse 190ft (58m) long and 136ft (41m) wide. It was built between 1860-62, replacing an earlier, much more modest, Corn Exchange built at the top of Briggate in 1827. It is constructed of local gritstone and a special feature of the building is the way that the stones that cover the outer walls and surround the round-headed windows are cut. In most local guides they are described as diamond-shaped stones, but in fact they are more like large pyramid-shaped blocks laid on their sides. Between the tops of the windows at the upper level are carved stone rosettes. Inside there were originally 59 offices at two levels for the millers, brewers, maltsters and other traders, placed all the way round the outer edge of the oval interior, those on the upper floor being entered from a balcony. The Exchange has been lovingly restored and is now an up-market shopping centre that also hosts exhibitions, fashion shows and musical events.

The glass dome, which rises 75ft (23m) above the main floor, means that bright light enters the building from above – critical when grain was being inspected and bought in large quantities on the trading floor. At one end of the interior beneath the great dome is a clock (right) framed on each side by standing sheaves of corn. At the other end is the familiar Leeds coat of arms (left) with its three stars from Mayor Thomas Danby's coat of arms, the owls from alderman Sir John Savile's coat of arms and the hanging fleece. Beneath is the motto *Pro Rege et Lege* – "For King and the Law".

Duncan Street, Corn Exchange and City Market

This panoramic view takes in the scene from the eastern end of a busy Duncan Street (on the left) and looks towards Vicar Lane and the City Market with its brick façade surmounted by chimneys, copper domes and steeple. On the right in the middle ground stands the Corn Exchange in splendid isolation between Call Lane, Cloth Hall Street and Crown Street.

The Headrow

This view of the Headrow (left) looks westwards towards Westgate with the Corinthian columns of the eastern façade of the Town Hall across Calverley Street visible through the trees. The Headrow was the main east-west route through early Leeds. It was widened by Leeds town planners between 1928-32 creating the wide modern street. In 1936-37 Victoria Square in front of the Town Hall was re-designed and enlarged and the war memorial moved there from City Square.

Town Hall

This magnificent edifice, like the Corn Exchange, was the work of Cuthbert Brodrick who was still only in his early thirties when he won the competition to design it. It was completed in 1858 and opened by Queen Victoria in September of that year. It is a solid and confident flagship of a proud Victorian city on the move. A wide flight of steps, flanked by lions, leads up to a central portico with 10 Corinthian columns. The building is topped by a magnificent colonnaded and domed clock tower rising to 225ft (69m). Inside a vestibule leads to the magnificent Victoria Hall.

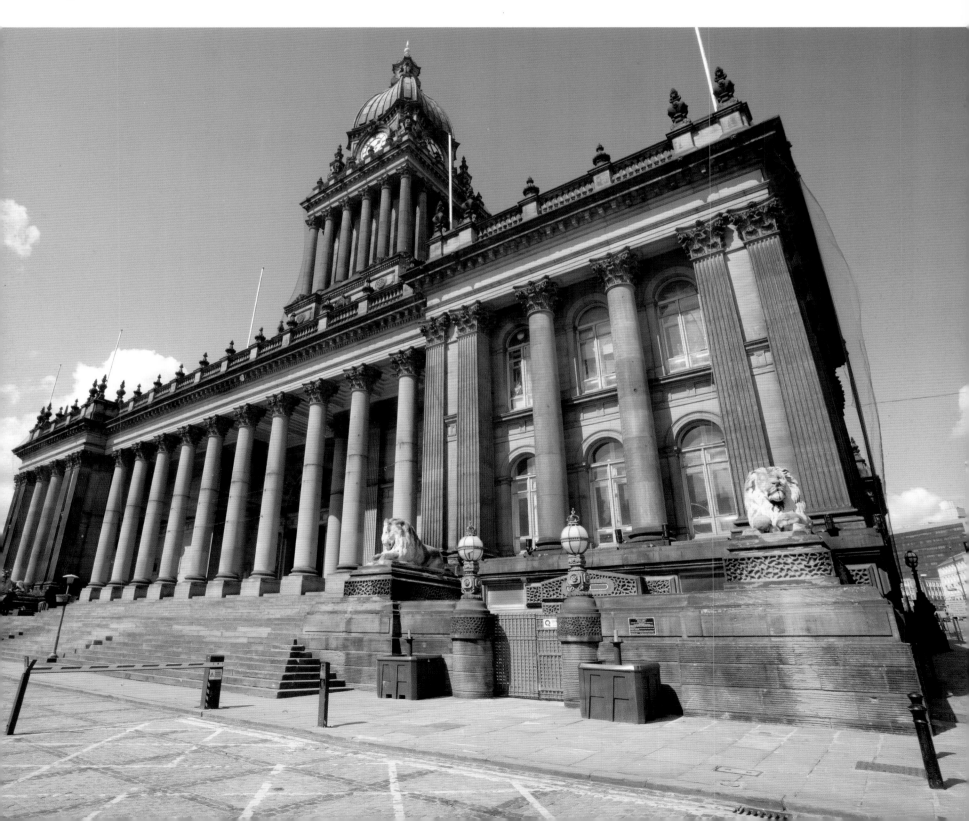

Municipal Buildings: Library and Art Gallery

Beside the Town Hall, across Calverley Street also overlooking the Headrow, are the Municipal Buildings designed in 1876 by George Corson and constructed between 1878-1884. The group consists of the old School Board building behind the Headrow between Alexander Street and Great George Street and fronting on to Calverley Street, and what were originally the municipal offices and library, now just the Central Library, beside the Headrow (right and far right). Beside the library is the City Art Gallery, opened in 1888, with a Henry Moore sculpture, *Reclining Woman* (1980), at the entrance.

The Tiled Hall

Of particular interest on the ground floor in the Municipal Buildings is the former Reading Room in the library, now the café and shop of the City Art Gallery and Central Library. The interior of this room (see photograph on the next page) is sumptuously decorated. It is flanked by shining granite columns. Tiled walls lead to a vaulted ceiling beautifully decorated with dazzling, intricate patterns of multi-coloured glazed bricks. So beautiful was the ceiling that it was feared that people would be continually gazing at it in wonder and not be able to concentrate on reading the newspapers and magazines. The floor is parquet and, like the ceiling, is also intricately patterned in oak, ebony and walnut.

Library & War Memorial

The general view (above) is from Victoria Gardens looking west from near the southern end of Cookridge Street towards the Town Hall, Central Library, Art Gallery and Henry Moore Institute. In the right background can be seen the war memorial (close-up right). The stone war memorial, which dates from 1922, is in Carrara marble with St George slaying a dragon on one side and a woman releasing a dove of peace on the other. On top is a recent statue of a winged figure of peace that replaced an earlier statue of Victory, removed in the 1960s. The memorial was originally sited in City Square and was moved to its present location in 1937.

Oxford Place

Beside the Town Hall is Oxford Place with the Methodist Church and beside it Oxford Chambers. The church, on the left, which dates from 1896-1903, is in a late Victorian Baroque style. Constructed of red brick and sandstone there is a fine entrance flanked by double-decked Ionic columns. At roof level there is a shapely central gable and at each of the front corners a cupola. Next door to the church, Oxford Chambers is in the same style and materials. Linking the two buildings is a tall, cupola-surmounted tower. Voluntary organisations including Christian Aid and International Voluntary Service occupy Oxford Chambers.

Nuffield Hospital & Centaur House

To the west of the Town Hall north of Westgate lies another group of important public buildings. On Leighton Street, adjacent to Leeds General Infirmary, is the Nuffield Hospital (right) completed in 2002. This 11-storey private hospital contains 80 bedrooms and six operating theatres. On the south side of Great George Street beside the hospital (on the far right in the photograph) is the former Centaur Clothing Factory, converted in 1999. It now contains 33 loft-style apartments and eight penthouses. Between Nuffield Hospital and Centaur House, commissioned by the hospital in 2002, is a group of four white figures by Faith Babbington entitled *The Human Spirit*.

Magistrates' Court

On the north side of Westgate between Leighton Street and Park Street is Leeds Magistrates' Court, completed in 1994. Through the porched and pedimented entrance, above which is the official coat of arms of the United Kingdom of Great Britain and Northern Ireland, is an atrium with gold-flecked walls. There are courtrooms on five floors furnished in woods that increasingly lighten in colour with each floor. The Leeds owl occurs at various points in the building.

Combined Courts Centre

The Combined Courts Centre is also on Westgate, between the Town Hall and the Magistrates' Court. It is so-named because under one roof is the High Court and Crown Court of Leeds, the District Registry of the High Court of Justice and Leeds County Court. Its location extends the old civic quarter westwards and conveniently across the Headrow is that part of Leeds city centre that has a large number of legal firms. Constructed out of red brick, it is a solid, functional building, only a few storeys high. Inside there is a central hall surrounded by courtrooms and offices.

Leeds Permanent, "The Light"

To the east of the Municipal Buildings still on the north side of the Headrow is the former headquarters of the Leeds Permanent Building Society (Permanent House and the Headrow Buildings). The building society moved headquarters in the 1990s and the building was used for some time by Leeds City Council before being redeveloped and re-opened as a retail and leisure centre in 2001-02. It is called "The Light" after the title of the in-house newspaper issued to its employees by the Leeds Permanent Building Society. It contains shops, bars and restaurants, a fitness club, a 13-screen cinema and a hotel.

The Radisson Hotel

The elegant Radisson Hotel is located in the Cookridge Street elevation of Permanent House which was restored in 2002. The hotel contains 147 rooms and has two floors of conference facilities. The architecture of the whole block, the facade along the Headrow and the extension up Cookridge Street which dates from the early 1930s with extensions in the 1950s is of the same materials, brick and Portland stone.

The Light

The Light has more than 344,445sq ft (32,000sq m) of retail space. It is on four levels: the courtyard level, the arcade level, the balcony level and the upper balcony level connected by escalators. The centre incorporates a glazed roof high above the former Upper Fountaine Street, which gives it the appearance of a late 20th century version of the earlier Victorian and Edwardian shopping arcades.

St Anne's

St Anne's, Leeds' Roman Catholic cathedral, was built between 1901-04 to replace an earlier church that was demolished during a road-widening scheme. It became a cathedral in 1924. It is in the Arts & Crafts Gothic style. At the west front, facing Cookridge Street, above the entrance is a sculpture (below) representing the crucifixion of Christ. On the north side facing George Street is the tall, three-stage tower. The interior of the cathedral is high and wide and there is a strong sense of space. One of the treasures of St Anne's is a *reredos* (an ornamental structure behind and above an altar) in the Lady Chapel (right). This is by the great Victorian architect, draughtsman and writer Augustus Pugin, best-known for his contribution with the architect Sir Charles Barry to the design of the Houses of Parliament and for his designs for their decoration and furnishing. The reredos was designed by Pugin in 1842 and was originally in the old St Anne's church that was demolished. It shows the Virgin Mary in the centre with, at either end, St Anne and St Wilfrid, and six smaller figures in between. It is painted in blue, red and gold.

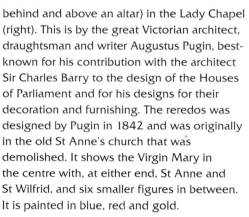

The Merrion Centre

The Merrion Shopping Centre in Merrion Street (bottom centre) between Woodhouse Lane and Wade Lane was opened in 1964. The design integrated on the same site a pedestrianised shopping precinct (at first open to the skies but later enclosed as shown below), a nightclub, dance hall, cinema and car parking. The cinema, the Odeon, closed in 1977. The centre now includes a Morrison's superstore, a bowling alley and several public houses.

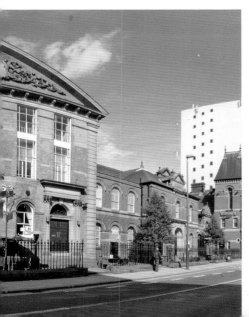

Bond Court

To the west of Park Row and to the south of
Russell Street is Bond Court (above), a small,
quiet backwater free of traffic in the centre
of the city. Shady cherry trees and tables and
chairs on which shoppers and office workers
can sit and rest or have a picnic lunch in the
summer add a note of calm to the scene.
Completing the picture is a group of bronze
figures by Roger Burnett playing *boules*.

Park Square

Across the Headrow to the south-west
of the Town Hall lies another square, Park
Square (right), this time with a lawned area
and formal planting. Across the lawn can
be seen the roof-line of St Paul's House,
originally built as a factory and warehouse
for Sir John Barran (1821-1905) the
pioneering manufacturer of ready-made
clothing and prominent Leeds citizen (he was
mayor twice and also served as Liberal MP).
The building, in brick and terracotta, was
completed in 1878 and is in the Moorish
style. Clearly visible are the pierced parapet
and two of the (replacement) small minarets.
It was converted into offices in 1976.

Park Square town houses

The surviving town houses in Park Square are of great architectural and social interest. Begun in 1788 and completed in 1794, Park Square is the only Georgian residential square to be built in the city and was once the home of gentlemen, lawyers, merchants and surgeons. Converted into offices and other non-residential uses in the 19th century, some are again private houses. One of the finest houses in the square is No 41 (below) built for a lawyer, William Bolland. Vicarage Chambers (left) was the vicarage of St Paul's church which once stood on the south side of the square.

Millennium Square and the Civic Hall

In 1999-2000 Millennium Square replaced the gardens that had been created in front of the Civic Hall in 1933. The Civic Hall was designed by E Vincent Harris (1879-1971) the Devon-born architect who was responsible for a number of public buildings in Britain mainly in the inter-war period, including Sheffield City Hall, Manchester Central Library and Surrey County Hall. The style is Palladian and the building material is Portland stone. The façade is symmetrical with a central portico with four large Corinthian columns supporting the pediment. Tall slim towers with spires on top rise from each end of the façade.

Civic pride

The ornamentation of the Civic Hall has many clues which link it firmly to Leeds and its history. There is a carved Leeds coat of arms in the pediment and clocks by William Potts & Son are fixed on brackets. But the most obvious and amusing signs of a Leeds location are the gilded owls, based on the owls in the city's coat of arms. Two sit on tall pedestals in front of the Civic Hall and they appear again on top of the spires looking down into the square.

Leeds General Infirmary

The original building fronting onto Great George Street (part of which is shown on the left) was designed by Sir George Gilbert Scott and built between 1863 and 1869 in the Gothic style. The building materials are brick with sandstone dressings. Scott visited hospitals on the Continent before tackling the design and he had the advice of Florence Nightingale who suggested that the hospital should have, among other things, an ice house and a chapel and wards that allowed good light and fresh air into them. The infirmary was enlarged in the 1890s by George Corson who had designed the Municipal Buildings, and other additions have been made since.

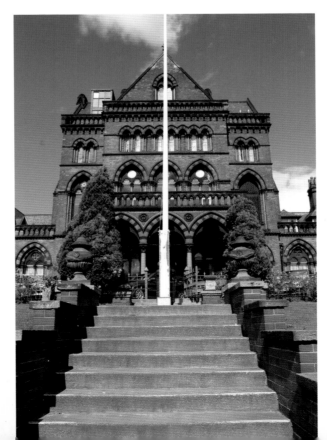

The Black Prince

Dominating the centre of City Square is a statue of the Black Prince. This was a gift from Colonel T Walter Harding, mayor of Leeds in 1899. It was designed by Thomas Brock, made in Belgium and transported to the city from the coast by water via the Humber and the Aire & Calder Navigation. The Black Prince has no connection with Leeds whatsoever. But this fact did not trouble Harding who believed that because the prince enshrined the chivalric ideal and brought back national pride to the English as a result of his victories during the Hundred Years War that he might also act as an inspiration to the people of Leeds.

City Square

This open space was created in the decade between 1893 and 1903 to celebrate the elevation of the town of Leeds to city status by the then mayor, Colonel T Walter Harding. The square was re-designed in 2002 by the civic architect, John Thorp, when the fountains were installed. In the panoramic photograph left looking east towards Boar Lane, the skyline is dominated by No 1 Park Row with its octagonal copper dome, the Mill Hill Unitarian Chapel, City Exchange offices, Park Plaza Hotel (a re-clad office building) and Queen's Hotel, which fronts the City Station and was built in 1937 by the LMS railway company architect. Below, City Square at night looking in the direction of the old General Post Office.

55

Princes Exchange, Princes Square

Princes Exchange is typical of the many new business premises that have appeared in Leeds over the last 20 years. It was designed by Carey Jones Architects and opened in 1999. It occupies a prime location in Princes Square between Wellington Street and the river Aire just a few minutes away from Leeds City Station, with easy access from the M1 and M62 and only 20 minutes from Leeds Bradford airport. Its tall glass profile makes it look like an ocean liner at anchor at the dockside, an image enhanced when it is lit up in darkness.

Leeds City Station

Leeds City Station dates from 1938, and is an amalgamation of the pre-existing New Station and Wellington Station. Originally Leeds had four separate stations; final amalgamation into one central station did not occur until the late 1930s. The new Queen's Hotel which fronts the station on City Square was re-built at the same time to replace a Victorian hotel of the same name. The station was virtually re-built in 1960. The station concourse, which was refurbished in 1999, is large and impressive to the first-time visitor. The roof over the platforms was reconstructed in 2001-03.

Hotel Metropole

Located in King Street in the heart of the city centre is the 120-bedroom former Hotel Metropole, now "The Met". This Grade II listed building has recently undergone a major refurbishment programme. It was designed by Chorley, Connon & Chorley and built between 1897-99. It is flamboyant in style with features borrowed from the château architecture of the Loire valley. An attractive feature of the building is the bowed entrance. The hotel is surmounted by a large stone cupola taken from the town's fourth White Cloth Hall that formerly occupied the site and which is commemorated in the blue plaque. An outstanding feature of the exterior of the hotel is the use of dusty-red terracotta (one of the best examples of terracotta work in Leeds) for the main wall-facings and architectural details such as the intricate decorative patterns at the hotel entrance. On the columns, over the door and on the pediment are acanthus leaves, female heads, bows and tassels, cherubs and swags of greenery and bunches of fruit. The cast-iron railings reflect the decorative work on the building by incorporating acanthus leaves in their design.

BBC and Leeds College of Music

In what may be called a "cultural quarter" between the Headrow and Quarry Hill lie the West Yorkshire Playhouse, the new headquarters for the Yorkshire region of the BBC and Leeds College of Music. The modern BBC premises, opened in 2004, are well-known to TV viewers throughout the Yorkshire region as the source of *Look North,* the regional news programme. Next to the curved and glass-fronted BBC premises stands the much plainer Leeds College of Music, one of the UK's leading centres of music education.

Grand Theatre

This building is really very grand. Before the performance on opening night in November 1878 of Shakespeare's *Much Ado About Nothing* the manager welcomed the audience to "one of the finest, if not the finest theatre in Europe". It was designed by George Corson, the architect of the Municipal Buildings, assisted by JR Watson. It is built in a mixture of the Romanesque and Gothic styles in brick and stone. Inside, the auditorium, which seats 2,600, is magnificent. A highly decorated proscenium arch is flanked by ornate boxes and above is a richly decorated ceiling. The theatre is the home of Opera North.

PART TWO

THE WATERFONT

This was Leeds' dockland area at the termini of the Aire and Calder Navigation and the Leeds and Liverpool Canal. It was also an important industrial area. By the 1960s the area was rundown and partially derelict. The city had turned its back on what had been a vital artery and hive of activity during its rise as a major centre of manufacturing. It has now been transformed, primarily through the enterprise of the Leeds Development Corporation working with both the City Council and the private sector. Existing but often semi-derelict warehouses have been converted into flats and offices and new riverside apartments, office buildings, café bars and restaurants have been built. The restoration of historic buildings and the construction of new ones have added a new and exciting dimension not only to the cityscape, but also to the residential, economic and leisure life of the city. From being a transport artery and then for many years a backwater, the Waterfront has now been grafted on to the booming central area of the city. Not surprisingly, with its phoenix-like rise from the ashes of neglect, stagnation and decline, the Waterfront area has been dubbed "Leeds-upon-Aire".

Leeds-upon-Aire

The scenes on these two pages show the way that old and new stand side by side on the Waterfront. The image to the right looks west along the river Aire. On the south bank of the river (on the left) are the Asda Headquarters built in 1988, one of the very first new developments on the decayed riverside. Opposite on the northern bank is Victoria Mills, a converted warehouse. In the background soars the 32-storey Bridgewater Place. Opened in April 2007, it boasts 10 floors of office space and 200 apartments on the upper 20 floors.

Victoria Mills

The view at the bottom left looks west over new and refurbished waterfront premises, with the tower of St Peter's parish church on Kirkgate in the background. The once busy and noisy riverside is now a calm oasis for residents. Below is the refurbished five-storey Victoria Mills, with its carved datestone, 1836, still surviving at the very apex of the building. Beyond are new apartment buildings more or less sympathetically designed in a warehouse/waterside mill style with their gables facing the water's edge.

Dock Street

This street is unusual in that it contains original dockside buildings mainly dating from the late 18th century to the early 20th century. On the north side, for example, are the recently refurbished Navigation Offices of 1906 and old warehouses that have been converted into residential space. On the south side are merchants' houses, warehouses and workshops. These include a brick-built gabled warehouse (above) with still, after tasteful refurbishment, two round arched entrances for horse transport and, high on the wall, loading bay doors.

Granary Wharf

Granary Wharf (right) is the modern name for the Leeds-Liverpool Canal wharf at its terminus in Leeds. Construction began in 1770. The first stretch of the canal from Leeds to Gargrave in Airedale was completed in 1777, but the very long canal was not completed to its Liverpool terminus until 1816. Today, Yorkshire Hire Cruisers operate a narrowboat service from Granary Wharf. *The Kirkstall Flyboat* is a purpose-built pleasurecraft, popular for celebrations and weekend cruises.

Design Innovation Centre

Located to the east of Centenary Bridge on the northern side
of the river, the Design Innovation Centre (above) was
converted in 1988, one of the earliest schemes carried out
on the Waterfront. It was formerly a grain and flour warehouse.
An interesting feature of the conversion is the addition,
overlooking the river, of balconies that look like the modern
equivalents in glass, steel and timber of loading bays. There is
also a communal balcony overlooking the river at ground level.
The design received an RIBA Regional Award for Architecture.

Granary Wharf House

Sitting sedately near the Leeds and Liverpool Canal towards
the end of Water Lane, beside its giant neighbour, Bridgewater
Place, is Granary Wharf House, occupied by the Medical
Protection Society. This completely new three-storey building,
like most of its neighbours, is in red brick and was completed
in April 1994. It is designed in a restrained style with a slightly
projecting three-bay central entrance section surmounted at
roof level by a pediment.

Brewery Wharf

On the south bank of the river between the Centenary footbridge and Crown Point Bridge is the prestigious new development at Brewery Wharf with its offices, hotel, café bars, restaurants and 360 apartments. The development includes a three-storey rotunda designed by Carey Jones Architects. Brewery Wharf takes its name from Tetley's Brewery (since 1988 part of the Carlsberg Group) which occupies land on either side of Hunslet Lane. Joshua Tetley's name ranks with those of Michael Marks, Montague Burton, Benjamin Gott and Matthew Murray in the hall of fame of Leeds

entrepreneurs. He started business as a maltster but in 1822 he leased the small brewery of William Sykes in Salem Place just south of Brewery Wharf. By 1864 his son had bought the brewery and embarked on an ambitious expansion scheme, taking on local architect George Corson to design new maltings, hop store and fermenting room. The Brewery Wharf development encapsulates all that has made the Waterfront so attractive. For those who flock to the area keen on the idea of urban living and who work in the city centre it has all the advantages: location, access and style.

Brewery Wharf is centrally located not only within the waterfront area (with easy pedestrian cross-river access via the Centenary footbridge) but also within Leeds city centre with thousands of workplaces, big city and up-market shopping and entertainment just a few minutes away. And within and around the development itself there are places to eat and drink and enjoy the revived riverside environment with its formal planting and public art. Serviced modern office space and ample car parking provision near to the M1 and M62 plus a mainline railway station make for an attractive business environment.

Whitehall Riverside

Although much of the Waterfront development and redevelopment has taken place to the east of Victoria Bridge on Neville Street there have also been some interesting developments to the west on land formerly occupied by factories. Whitehall Riverside between Whitehall Road and the river Aire, which has seen some interesting development since the late 1990s, is a case in point. Smart new buildings here include No 1 Whitehall Riverside with 129,000sq ft (11,985sq m) of office space overlooking the river. More recently, fashionable multi-storey waterfront apartments have also been built in brick, aluminium and glass.

Centenary Footbridge

The Centenary footbridge crosses the river Aire halfway between Leeds Bridge and Crown Point Bridge and connects the eastern end of Dock Street on the south bank of the river with The Calls on the north bank. The bridge, which dates from 1992-1993, was designed by Ove Arup & Partners. It is a suspension bridge with just one support tower (bottom right) anchored on the south bank. It was the first bridge to be built across the river Aire near the city centre for more than a century. There are excellent views from the bridge of the waterfront area both upstream and downstream. In the panoramic image below, looking downstream, the Brewery Wharf development is just in view on the extreme right.

Langton's Wharf

Beyond the Design Innovation Centre on the northern bank of the river Aire stretching as far as Crown Point Bridge lie Langton's Wharf and Chandler's Wharf along the narrow riverside street, The Calls. Here again, as elsewhere along the Waterfront, new developments and sympathetic restorations and conversions can be seen side by side. Modern riverside housing at Langton's Wharf, as is clearly shown in the panoramic view below, is four-storeyed, and brick-built in the warehouse style with small windows and attractive balconies. Also in view, behind Langton's Wharf on Kirkgate, rises the battlemented and pinnacled tower of St Peter's parish church – in stark contrast to the modern riverside developments.

Chandler's Wharf

The name Chandler is redolent of a dockside location. A chandler was a dealer in oil, soap and paint, a corn chandler was a grain dealer and a ship's chandler dealt in cordage and canvas. The scene today along the river is very different from that shown in photographs of the riverside a century ago. Then it was smoky, with the river full of barges with armies of men loading and unloading goods onto carts. Today the riverside is calm, quiet and unpolluted.

Chandler's Wharf includes another interesting conversion (right and below) from working premises to housing. This time it is the brick-built warehouses and stables of William Turton's business which was founded in 1844. Turton provided feed for the horses used to pull the barges along the waterway. The complex includes a tall tower cleverly included in the modern conversion.

River crossings became more and more important as Leeds expanded in the Victorian period. As already noted

Leeds Bridge was replaced between 1870 and 1873, Victoria Bridge was constructed between 1837-39 and Crown Point Bridge (above and below) was constructed between 1840-1842. This single-span cast-iron bridge was made at the Park Iron Works in Sheffield. The bridge rails have a fine herringbone pattern. The bridge was repaired, widened and restored in 1994.

Clarence Dock and the Royal Armouries Museum

The panoramic view above looks north along Clarence Dock towards the river Aire and the city centre beyond. This large, stone-walled dock was opened in 1843 in anticipation of increased and continued competition from the railways - the Leeds to Selby railway had been opened in 1834 and meant there was a much quicker railway route to the east coast from Selby than by slow narrowboat on the Aire and Calder Navigation. Today, although there are still narrowboats tied up in the dock, they are leisure craft not commercial craft and they are completely surrounded by late 20th and 21st century developments. On the right is the Royal Armouries Museum and on the left is the brand-new £200m Clarence Dock mixed-use development including apartments, offices and shops. One of the biggest developments in the city, the Clarence Dock development is made up of four residential blocks, with each one designed to incorporate car parking, bars, cafés and restaurants at the lower levels. The first residential block, Magellan House (seen at the centre of the panoramic view and on the left) consists of 185 one- and two-bedroom flats and nine penthouses.

The Royal Armouries Museum (left and above) relocated from London to Leeds and opened in 1996 between the dock and the river. This national museum of arms and armour, formerly housed in the Tower of London, has 8,000 objects on permanent display with five themed galleries: War, Tournament, Self-Defence, Hunting, and Arms & Armour of the Orient. Jousting exhibitions, falconry and displays of horsemanship take place in the adjoining tiltyard.

The changing skyline of Leeds' Waterfront: the 32-storey Bridgewater Place, nicknamed "The Dalek", opened in April 2007

PART THREE
THE INNER CITY

The inner city in all large metropolitan areas, lying beyond the civic, retail and commercial heart, is commonly a very mixed area. Two of its main elements are the remains of the once solid ring of tightly packed inner residential areas, now radically altered due to redevelopment and road-building and widening, and industrial ribbons and clusters beside the waterways, railways and main roads. But it also contains other important land uses, some originally requiring a location as near as possible to the city centre, for example, university and college campuses, and others requiring large spaces such as sports grounds. Mingled among these inner city land uses, ancient place names and a surprising number of architectural gems suggest a history as long and as interesting as the city centre itself.

Inner city Leeds has all these elements in plenty. It has places with ancient names such as Armley, Bramley and Burmantofts, a fine Victorian church, wonderful industrial relics like the Temple Mills, Holbeck Towers and the Round Foundry, the houses of prominent Leeds industrialists, an early cemetery full of interesting monuments, two universities, a wonderful Edwardian pub and a gorgeous pre-First World War picture house.

Back to the future in inner city Leeds where buildings range from 21st century to late Georgian. From the top, clockwise: Tower Works; Round Foundry Media Centre; Denison Hall; Temple Mills; the Innovation Hub, University of Leeds. This cutting-edge building by Carey Jones Architects opened in September 2007 and is adjacent to the Leeds innovation centre and the business school. It provides office space and support to new businesses in health and the biosciences.

University of Leeds

The University of Leeds was originally the Yorkshire College of Science then, with colleges in Manchester and Liverpool, it became part of the federal Victoria University in 1887 and finally the University of Leeds in 1904. It was the threat that Victoria University College in Leeds might become the University of Yorkshire that spurred on its Yorkshire rival Sheffield to gain its full university charter in 1905. The university campus occupies a large triangular area immediately north-west of the city centre between Clarendon Road in the west and south-west and Woodhouse Lane in the east. It has more than 7,000 staff and over 30,000 students.

A critical mix

University buildings have expanded over the site for more than a century and are in a variety of styles and materials. The Great Hall (left), completed in 1894, is by Alfred Waterhouse, also known for his designs for university buildings in Manchester and Liverpool, and the Natural History Museum and University College Hospital in London. Built in brick and stone the main external features are the large

Perpendicular-style window between two towers topped by spires. In a completely different style and of a different building material is the Parkinson Building (above, and below at night). Built of Portland stone with its landmark tower, it is named after its major donor, Frank Parkinson, a former student, who began his studies in electrical engineering in 1908 and who became chairman of Compton Parkinson,

electrical goods manufacturers. The building was officially opened by the Princess Royal in 1951. In complete contrast again is the University of Leeds Business School on Moorland Road (bottom p80), housed in the former Leeds Grammar School. Looking more like a medieval church than a business school it was built in 1858-59. The glass-covered arcade alongside the building was added in 2001.

Leeds – the university town

The combined inner city campuses of the University of Leeds and Leeds Metropolitan University, which stretch from Clarendon Road in the west to the edge of the city centre in the east, form a compact university town within the City of Leeds. They have a combined student population of more than 60,000. Both are outstanding research and teaching institutions. The University of Leeds is in the top ten of British universities in terms of the research funding that it attracts. Graduates of the university include aviation pioneer Robert Blackburn, Nobel prizewinner George Porter, sociologist Richard Hoggart, writer Storm Jameson and Labour politicians Jack Straw and Clare Short. Leeds Metropolitan University has been praised for keeping its student fees well below the maximum level. Most of its students are from the surrounding region and in 2006 it won the award for the "outstanding contribution to the local community" at the annual higher education awards ceremony sponsored by the *Times Higher Education Supplement.*

Below is the reading room at the Brotherton Library at the University of Leeds. This magnificent space for reading and research has a diameter of 160ft (49m) and is encircled by green marble columns that support a dome. Opened in 1936, it was the gift of the chemical manufacturer Lord Brotherton of Wakefield (1856-1930) who donated £100,000 for its construction.

Leeds Metropolitan University

This institution, which received its university charter in 1992, was formerly Leeds Polytechnic formed in 1970 through the amalgamation of four existing colleges. In 1976 James Graham College and the City of Leeds and Carnegie College of Physical Education also joined Leeds Polytechnic. In addition to its central campus, Leeds Metropolitan University also has a suburban campus in Headingley split between Beckett Park and the Carnegie Stand at Headingley Carnegie Stadium which contains 12 teaching rooms and a large meeting room. In 1998 the university merged with Harrogate College to form a Harrogate campus.

The city campus combines purpose-built modern buildings (below) and conversions of older buildings to university use. Among purpose-built university accommodation are the former polytechnic buildings between Calverley Street and Woodhouse Lane, including alterations and modernisations such as the Leslie Silver Building (1999-2000). Among other acquisitions are Cloth Hall Court, the old Broadcasting House, the former Leeds headquarters of the BBC, and most of Queen Square (left) a quiet backwater of brick, early 19th century houses.

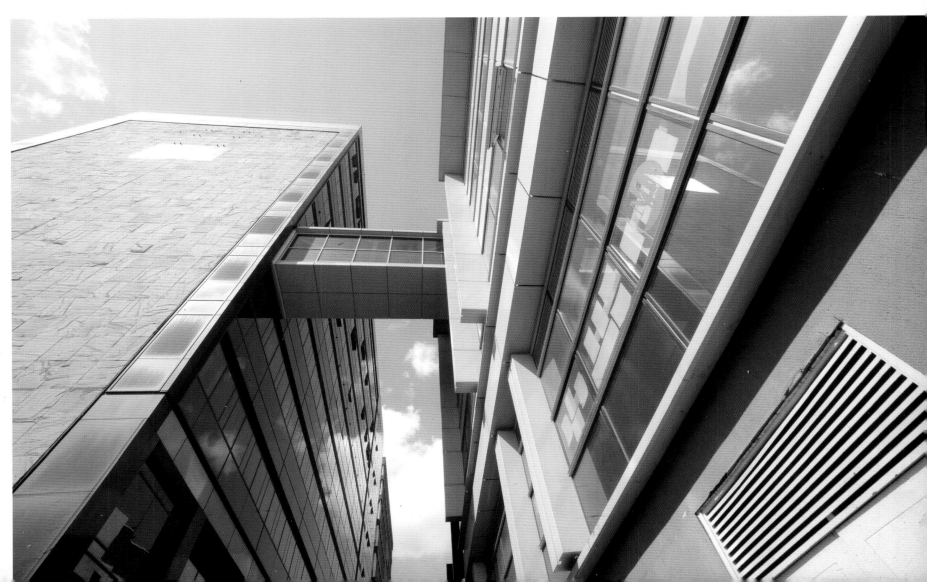

Denison Hall

Situated conspicuously at the north-west corner of Hanover Square to the west of the University of Leeds campus is Denison Hall, the late 18th century house of rich wool merchant John Wilkinson Denison. Still elegant, although now converted into flats, it is three-storeyed and has five bays with bow-fronted wings on either side. The façade is capped by a pediment with three urns on top. Hanover Square was once part of the grounds of the house.

Hyde Park Picture House

It is only when the modern visitor can carefully inspect an early surviving cinema that it becomes clear why they were called "picture palaces". Many, of course, were designed in a Moorish style and given exotic names like the "Alhambra". This is not the case with Hyde Park Picture House on Brudenell Road which dates from 1914. It has a plain name and the red brick exterior has a Dutch-looking gable above an entrance with imitation white marble columns. Inside many of the original fittings and arrangements have survived including the kiosk, the entrance lobby floor in a mosaic pattern and a vaulted auditorium (right) with a balcony decorated with swags of plasterwork.

Temple Mills

The former mills of John Marshall (1765-1843) lie to the south of Leeds City Station on Marshall Street in Holbeck. John Marshall inherited his father's linen drapery business in his early 20s and switched to flax-spinning and eventually to linen-weaving. His business was a runaway success and he became a very rich man.

In 1838 he engaged Joseph Bonomi, an Egyptologist, assisted it is thought by the painter David Roberts who had travelled in the Middle East, to design a new mill in the Egyptian style. The chimney was designed to resemble Cleopatra's needle. The weaving shed, which covers nearly two acres, has columns on the outside walls and cast-iron columns inside all decorated with the lotus (Egyptian water lily). The front of the block of offices (above) has six lotus columns and the walls have carvings of snakes, hieroglyphs and the sun.

Holbeck Towers

These tall brick towers rise above the Tower Works on Globe Road in Holbeck beside the Leeds and Liverpool Canal. This was the works developed by the Harding family, who were manufacturers of steel pins for use in textile machinery. The business closed in 1979. The chimneys, for that is what the towers are, are all inspired by medieval Italian towers. In the main photograph the tower on the right dates from 1864-66, the one in the middle from 1899 and the one on the left from 1920. The 1864-66 tower was designed by Thomas Shaw and was inspired by the Lamberti bell tower in Verona. The 1899 tower was by William Bakewell and is based on the Giotto campanile at the Duomo in Florence. The 1920 tower has the look of a Tuscan tower house. Also surviving on the site is an engine house with tiled walls that are decorated with plaster medallions with the portraits of famous inventors of textile machinery (including the Hardings). The Tower Works is currently undergoing refurbishment and conversion to office, residential and retail space as part of the Holbeck Urban Village project.

Garden Gate, Hunslet

Hunslet today is an industrial as well as residential suburb with a mixture of old industrial buildings, modern industrial estates, residential housing, terraces, villas and high rise blocks. But in a sea of ordinariness is one of the gems of Leeds, the famous public house called the Garden Gate. This Edwardian public house, which is complete in every detail, was called by the architectural writer Lynn F Pearson in her book *Building the West Riding* (1994) one of the best buildings in Leeds, adding that some people would say the very best. And yet it has been threatened by demolition on more than one occasion. It dates from 1902 and replaced an earlier public house on the same site. The architect is unknown but some writers believe it may be the work of Thomas Winn & Sons who were also responsible for the Hyde Park Picture House. The ground floor façade of the Garden Gate is decorated with a bronzy-brown covering of intricately patterned Burmantofts faience. Inside Edwardian tiling, glasswork and original joinery have all survived.

The Round Foundry

The Round Foundry in Water Lane, Holbeck was where the famous engineer Matthew Murray (1765-1826) set up his new works in 1795. Murray built his first steam engine in 1799, made many improvements to steam engine design, was the first to make machine tools and in 1812 manufactured the first commercially successful steam locomotive for the Middleton Colliery a few miles to the south. This locomotive did the work previously undertaken by 50 horses and 200 men. A painting of one of Murray's locomotives at Middleton Colliery is famously featured in George Walker's *Costumes of Yorkshire*, published in 1814.

The Media Centre

The Round Foundry complex, now the Round Foundry Media Centre, was the first major project undertaken as part of the Holbeck Urban Village project, designed to breathe new life into a part of Leeds that had once been the scene of industrial innovation and progress but which for many years had been suffering from neglect and decline. Completed in 2004 the media complex provides office space for businesses in the digital, media and creative industries. There is office space for up to 50 businesses together with apartments, bars and cafés. Good use has been made of surviving buildings and other structures to create an interesting new business environment.

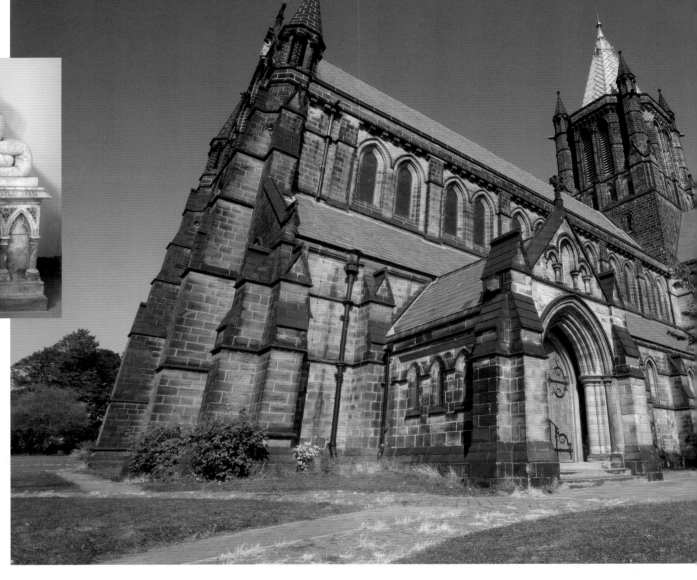

St Bartholomew's, Armley

This large sandstone church is one of Leeds' best Victorian churches. It was built between 1872-78 in the Early English style with the tower added in 1904. Inside it is very spacious and contains interesting Victorian carvings and a fine monument to Benjamin Gott (above). It was at this church in September 1928 that the vicar married the parents of the playwright Alan Bennett at 8am so that the groom would not be late for the start of his day's work in the butcher's at Lower Wortley Co-op at 8.15.

Armley House

This is now the clubhouse for the Gott's Park golf course, but it was once the home of the wealthy wool manufacturer Benjamin Gott (1762-1840). Gott is credited with building the world's first woollen factory at Bean Ings on the river Aire. Gott leased the Armley House estate from the previous owner and then in 1803 bought it and began to re-model the house and grounds. Humphrey Repton had worked up designs for both the house and grounds by 1810 and in 1816, after Gott had moved in permanently, Robert Smirke was retained to draw up plans to re-model the house in the Grecian style.

Bramley Forge Locks

Work started on the Leeds and Liverpool Canal in 1770 but it was 46 years before it was finished. On its completion the canal was 117 miles (187 km) in length – the longest in Britain. It was not only lengthy but on its trans-Pennine route it had to ascend and descend steep slopes. Altogether it is estimated that it climbs 487ft (148m) over the Pennines resulting in the frequent use of locks. Two of the best preserved on the Yorkshire side of the Pennines are in Leeds – the Newlay Locks and Bramley Forge locks (right), still plied by narrowboats.

Beckett Street Cemetery, Burmantofts

As industrial towns expanded rapidly in the 19th century (Leeds' population grew from 53,000 in 1801 to 429,000 in 1901) churchyards became overcrowded and then completely full. Beckett Street Cemetery in Burmantofts, originally called Leeds Township Cemetery, was the largest of three established in Leeds in the 1840s and more than 180,000 people were buried there. The cemetery was divided into two parts, one for Anglican burials and the other for Nonconformists. The cemetery chapels no longer survive but the late Victorian Tudor-style lodges still stand. The cemetery contains some very interesting Victorian monuments including one to a ship's captain who died in 1849 with a carving of a Humber keel, some splendid monuments to the Galli and Marks families and one to an old soldier who had taken part in the Charge of the Light Brigade during the Crimean War.

Elland Road

Elland Road became the home of Leeds United Football Club following the ejection from the Football League of their predecessors, Leeds City, for making illegal payments to players. Leeds United were elected to the Football League in 1920. The development of the ground has gone through a number of important stages. The first stand, the West Stand, was built in the days of the Leeds City club in 1905 and this was followed in the 1920s by the so-called Scratching Shed and Spion Kop. A new Kop (now the Don Revie Stand) was constructed in 1958 and in 1974 the Scratching Shed was replaced by the South Stand. The latest addition was the cantilever stand, the biggest in the world. The record attendance at the ground was 57,892

in a Cup tie against Sunderland in March 1967. The modern ground capacity is just over 40,000. Leeds United won the First Division Championship in 1968, 1974 and 1993 and the FA Cup in 1972. The greatest period in the club's history came in the Don Revie era of the 1960s and early 1970s. During the period when Revie was manager (1961-74) the club won the First Division Championship twice, the FA Cup once, the League Cup once and the European Fairs Cup twice. The array of outstanding players at the club during that period was almost endless including Billy Bremner (whose statue is shown on the right), Jack Charlton, Johnny Giles, Eddie Gray, Peter Lorimer, Alan Clarke and Norman Hunter.

PART FOUR
THE SUBURBS, SURROUNDING TOWNS & VILLAGES

Surrounding the city centre and the inner city are the middle and outer suburbs of Leeds that often have their own long histories. Embedded in these suburbs, now largely made up of rows of late 19th and early 20th century terrace houses, and more modern brick and slate detached and semi-detached houses, there is one fine medieval church, the ruins of a medieval abbey, a good number of handsome Victorian churches, stone villas and mansions of leading Leeds industrialists who had fled the smoky town in the 19th century for clearer air on the higher ground to the north, historic parkland, and old and new buildings that reflect the recently rapidly changing social geography of the suburban areas.

Beyond these suburbs stretches a wide area administered by Leeds City Council since 1974 that is now part of the metropolitan borough, and which takes in towns and villages that were once administered by the West Riding County Council. In these peripheral areas, with their still pretty villages and attractive market towns, there is a great mix of buildings and structures in Millstone Grit, Coal Measure Sandstone and Magnesian Limestone. These buildings include some magnificent country houses, fine medieval churches, sturdy early bridges, Georgian coaching inns and rows of beautiful almshouses.

Kirkstall Abbey

The ruins of Kirkstall Abbey lie just three miles north-west of the city centre. This abbey was founded in 1147 by monks and lay brothers from Fountains Abbey but they did not move to Leeds until 1152 when land was granted to them at what they called Kirkstall ("site of a church") by wealthy landowner Henry de Lacy. It is believed that the church was completed within 25 years.

At the Dissolution in 1539 the monastic community consisted of an abbot and 30 monks. In 1890 the site was bought from a private owner and presented to Leeds Corporation who undertook some building repairs before opening it as a public park in 1893.

Abbey House Museum

To the north of the main abbey site across Abbey Road is the inner gatehouse (below), for centuries used as a farmhouse, but which has housed the Abbey House Museum for many years. The Museum has recreated Victorian streets, an interactive gallery and tea rooms.

Although Kirkstall Abbey is in ruins, enough has survived to show clearly the plan of the original buildings. On the main site the church (left and right) still stands high with the cloisters to the south and beyond those the remains of the cellarer's range, kitchens, infirmary and the abbot's house. The site has recently seen the completion of a multi-million pound project which has included the opening of a new visitor centre, restoration of the ruins and landscaping of the grounds.

St John's, Adel

St John the Baptist's church in Adel in north Leeds is worth going a long way to see. It is among the
very best of Norman churches in Yorkshire. The small church is simple in plan with a nave, chancel,
with no tower or spire but with a bellcote built in the Victorian period to replace a previous one.
One of the treasures of the church is a stone corbel-table surrounding the walls of the church carved
into the heads of beasts and expressive human faces. The church also boasts a magnificent Norman
doorway with the archway carrying four rows of detailed carved decoration in the form of animals,
rolls, zigzags and beakheads. On the door is a replica (the original one was stolen) of a bronze
Norman door-ring (right) portraying a monster swallowing a man whose head is sticking out of
the monster's mouth.

Graveyard monuments

Adel churchyard has some interesting monuments, but in Lawnswood Cemetery, opened in 1875 to serve the growing suburbs of Headingley and Far Headingley, there are some stunning examples. The most unusual one (top right) is to Ethel Preston who died in 1911. A lady in Edwardian dress stands in a porch with Corinthian columns and a balustrade above, reputedly based on the porch of her home in Leeds. Behind her the door is deliberately left just open.

Chapeltown and Potter Newton

Chapeltown and its surrounding area has had the most colourful and rapidly changing social history of any of Leeds' residential districts. It developed in the 19th century as a new suburb for the lower middle classes who could reach the rapidly growing retail, commercial and still important manufacturing parts of the town (and after 1893, city) by tram. But the 20th century saw enormous and rapid changes in its social composition. First, Jewish families, who had come to Leeds from eastern Europe in large numbers in the three decades after 1880 moved to Chapeltown in the 1920s mainly from the Leylands and Little London areas to the south and the Jewish population of Chapeltown reached its peak in the 1940s. As they prospered in the post-war years they moved further north to the outer suburbs and their place was taken by other groups, mainly from the West Indies, India and Pakistan.

The buildings and the changing uses of buildings on Chapeltown Road in Chapeltown and neighbouring Potter Newton and Newton Park reflect the social changes of the area. The splendid shopping parade at 168-175 Chapeltown Road (above), for example, built in 1890, reflects the early phase of its suburban development. Two carved lions at each end look down in splendour. In complete contrast is the Northern School of Contemporary Dance (far left) which occupies the former United Hebrew Congregation Synagogue built between 1929-1932. Another building that has seen a change of use is the former Union Chapel (right) which became a Sikh temple before the building of the new temple (left) in yellow brick in 2000.

Gledhow Grove

Standing among more modern housing to the east of Harrogate Road, between Gledhow Park Road and Harehills Lane, is Gledhow Grove, built between 1835-40 for Leeds industrialist John Hives, partner in the still surviving flax-spinning Bank Mills on the north bank of the navigable river Aire to the west of the Royal Armouries site. In the Greek Revival style, this is a stately stone-built, two-storey mansion, 11 bays wide. Four tall columns, the outer two Doric, the inner two flanking the entrance, of the Ionic order are topped by a fine pediment. The building eventually became Chapel Allerton Hospital.

St Aidan's, Harehills

This big red brick church in the Italian Romanesque style in Roundhay Road, Harehills, was completed in 1894. It is the mosaics in the chancel that attract visitors to the building. They depict scenes from the life of St Aidan and are by the artist Sir Frank Brangwyn (1867-1956). They date from 1916. St Aidan was the founder and first bishop of the monastery on the island of Lindisfarne in Northumberland. He is credited with re-introducing Christianity to the region. He died in 651. The mosaics depict St Aidan feeding the poor, his arrival in Northumberland, St Aidan preaching and his death.

Roundhay Park

This 373-acre public park, the largest in Leeds, was opened in 1872, but its history as a park goes much further back than that. It was first mentioned in the 12th century when it was a deer park (hay = hedged deer enclosure) of the de Lacy family and part of the boundary ditch still survives in the north-east corner. In 1803 half of the former de Lacy Roundhay estate came into the hands of Thomas Nicholson, a banker, who landscaped the grounds and built the mansion which survives to this day. It now houses the park's visitor centre.

The Rotunda

Roundhay was bought from its private owner in 1871 by the Lord Mayor of Leeds, Sir John Barran, and a group of associates who then sold it to the Corporation. It was nicknamed "The Great White Elephant" until the electric trams reached it in the early 1890s allowing the ordinary folk of Leeds, crowded in the inner city to the south, to reach it quickly and cheaply. The Rotunda, a roofed drinking fountain, was a gift of Sir John Barran.

Lakes and a castle

The park underwent a major restoration in 2004. Among its attractions are two lakes, the 33-acre Waterloo Lake (left) which is fed from the north by a series of cascades and waterfalls and the smaller Upper Lake. There is also a sham medieval castle (above) which performed the function of a tea room for the Nicholson family. The park has a number of beautiful gardens: the Canal Gardens (extreme left) which contain a rectangular-shaped lake and are enclosed by a high wall, the Alhambra Garden, Monet Garden and the Coronation House (now Tropical World).

Headingley

People of means began to leave the centres of Britain's growing industrial towns at the end of the 18th century and the movement gathered pace during the 19th century. As many industrial towns developed along river valleys where water power and later canals and railways were routed, the better-off moved to higher ground away from the soot and smoke of the central areas. Headingley is a prime example of a suburb which developed on higher ground with good access to the centre via a turnpiked road (now Headingley Lane-Otley Road). The area is now full of Victorian villas, large and small (like the Lutheran Church House on Alma Road, above) along tree-lined streets, some still family homes but many converted into apartments and student accommodation. A typical example of the large villa and mansion development in Headingley in the 19th century is Headingley Castle (far right). Looking very grand with its three-storey tower and battlements, it was built between 1843-46 for a wealthy corn merchant. It is now converted into flats.

The rapid 19th century suburbanisation of Headingley was accompanied by the building of grand churches. St Michael's on Otley Road, completed in 1886, was by JL Pearson, best known for his designs for two cathedrals – Truro and Brisbane. Equally grand is St Augustine's (above right) at the southern end of Headingley Lane, this time in the Decorated style with a tall tower surmounted by an almost equally tall spire. Outside the church is a statue of Sir Robert Peel (left) that once stood outside the Court House in Park Row. It is perhaps appropriate that this advocate of free trade should stand at the southern gateway of this suburb created by Leeds' Victorian industrialists.

Headingley Stadium

Headingley Stadium, now Headingley Carnegie Stadium, is two sports grounds rolled into one. Headingley Cricket Ground is the headquarters of Yorkshire County Cricket Club and has been a Test Match ground since 1899 when England played a Test match against Australia. A host of legendary cricketers are associated with the club and the ground: Hedley Verity, Sir Leonard Hutton, Brian Close, Fred Trueman, Ray Illingworth, the Test umpire "Dickie" Bird, Geoffrey Boycott and Michael Vaughan, to name but a few. The ground has seen some memorable performances. In 1977 it was at Headingley that Geoff Boycott completed his 100th Test century. But more memorable still, perhaps, was England's fightback and eventual victory over Australia in 1981 when, in the second innings, Ian Botham scored a thrilling 149 not out and Bob Willis followed with a magnificent bowling performance of 8 for 43. In 2001 the Sir Leonard Hutton Gates (below) were installed and opened to commemorate the life and playing career of Pudsey-born Sir Len who retired from cricket in 1955 and died in 1990, aged 74.

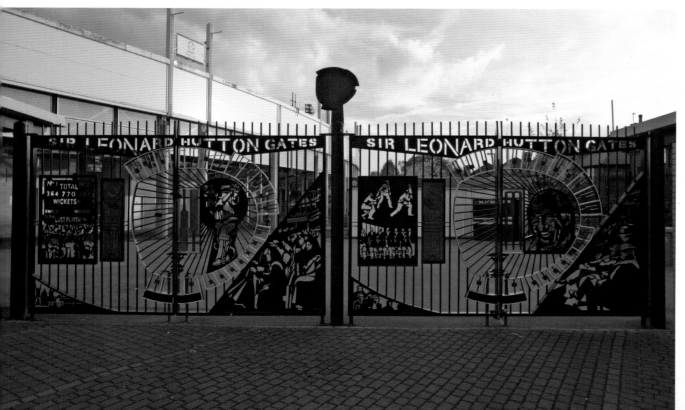

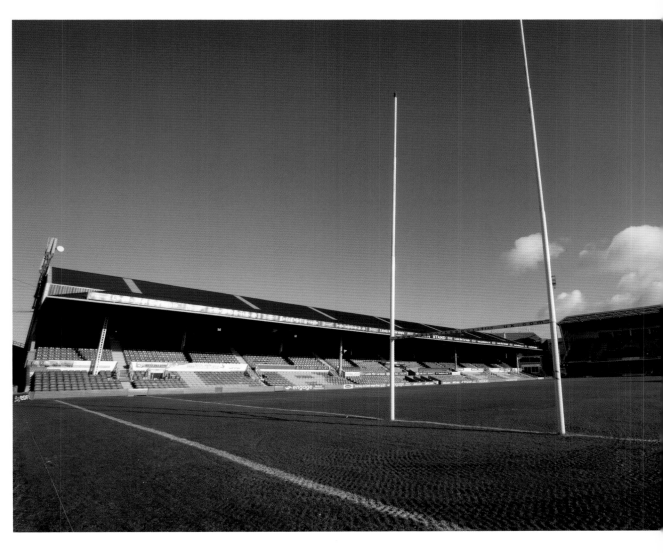

Leeds rugby

Next door to the cricket ground is a rugby stadium where rugby league team Leeds Rhinos and the rugby union team Leeds Carnegie (formerly Leeds Tykes) play their home games. The rugby ground is also an international rugby league stadium which has held a crowd of over 40,000.

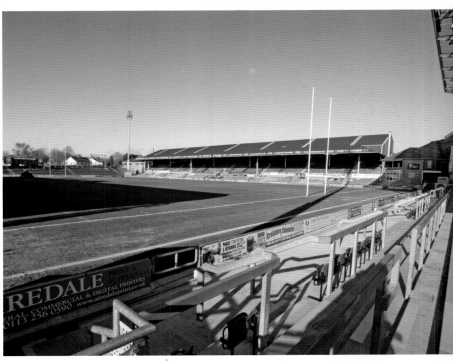

Temple Newsam

This grand 17th century house derives its name from the Knights Templar who held the manor from 1155 to 1312. There was a previous house on the site that belonged to Thomas, Lord Darcy, who was executed in 1537. The present house was built in brick in the Jacobean style in the 1620s or 1630s by Sir Arthur Ingram, whose descendants became the Viscounts Irwin. Sir Arthur was a London merchant who had become a very wealthy man through a series of royal appointments to James I and Charles I. His loyal sentiments are plain for all to see at the house. The following dedication (see photographs left and right) is picked out in letters around the balustrade in the courtyard: *All Glory and Praise be Given to God the Father the Son and Holy Ghost on High Peace on Earth Good Will Towards Men Honour and True Allegiance to Our Gracious King Loving Affection Amongst his Subjects Health and Plenty be Within this House.*

House and gardens

Temple Newsam, including more than 900 acres of gardens and surrounding parkland (landscaped by Capability Brown), was acquired by Leeds Corporation in 1922 from the Hon Edward Wood (later Lord Halifax). It was an empty house, the contents having been auctioned separately. The house became a museum and the grounds became a public park and golf course. The house is an outstanding museum of fine and decorative arts containing important collections of furniture, paintings, silver, porcelain, pottery, textiles and wallpapers including items that originally belonged to the house when it was in private ownership. In the house there are more than 30 rooms open to the public including the magnificent Great Hall and Picture Gallery. There are woodland, Italian and walled gardens, a home farm and a rare breeds collection. Guided tours, educational activities and special events (right) are a popular feature in the house and grounds.

Guiseley

Guiseley (the name means "Gislica's clearing") lies near the northern boundary of Leeds metropolitan borough south of Otley. It has a number of historical connections. Patrick Brontë and Maria Branwell, the parents of Anne, Charlotte and Emily Brontë were married in St Oswald's church. More recently, the town has gained fame because Harry Ramsden opened his first fish and chip restaurant in 1930 and it still survives (left). It is also claimed that Harry Corbett's puppet Sooty was "conceived" in another fish and chip shop in the town. Guiseley was also the home for 66 years (until 2002) of the factory that made Silver Cross prams.

Otley

Located on the north and south banks of the river Wharfe halfway between Bradford and Ilkley in the farming countryside of Wharfedale, Otley is a busy market town with a population of more than 14,000 at the 2001 census. There are spectacular views of the town from the Chevin (left), the gritstone escarpment to the south that rises to over 900ft (about 275m). In 1944 Major Horton Fawkes of nearby Farnley Hall donated more than 260 acres of the Chevin to the people of Otley. A royal charter to hold a market was granted in 1222 and cattle markets are also still held. The Otley Show, the oldest one-day agricultural show in the country, began in 1796. Held in May, it attracts about 15,000 visitors.

Otley

Most successful medieval market town grew up at river bridging points and Otley is no exception to this general rule. Still a major feature of the town is its stone-built medieval bridge (below) which made it accessible on market days to villagers living over a wide area of rich farming country to the north and south of the town. The bridge was re-built and widened after a flood in 1673.

The town has two splendid churches, one medieval and the other late Victorian. The medieval church is All Saints parish church (right). This has a late Norman north doorway and Norman windows in the chancel. The battlemented

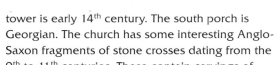

tower is early 14th century. The south porch is Georgian. The church has some interesting Anglo-Saxon fragments of stone crosses dating from the 9th to 11th centuries. These contain carvings of foliage and birds and beasts including a dragon. There are also interesting monuments in the church to local families including an early 17th century monument with a corpse wrapped in a shroud to William Vavassour and another with lying figures to Thomas Fairfax who died in 1640. In the churchyard at All Saints church there is a monument to the 23 railway navvies killed during the construction of the Bramhope Tunnel to the south-east of the town between 1845-49. It is in the form of a scaled-down version of the tunnel with the tunnel entrance at each end (inset above left).

The Victorian church is the Congregational church (top right) constructed in 1899, designed by the Bradford architects Thomas and Francis Healey. It is in the Gothic style with a tower surmounted by a spire.

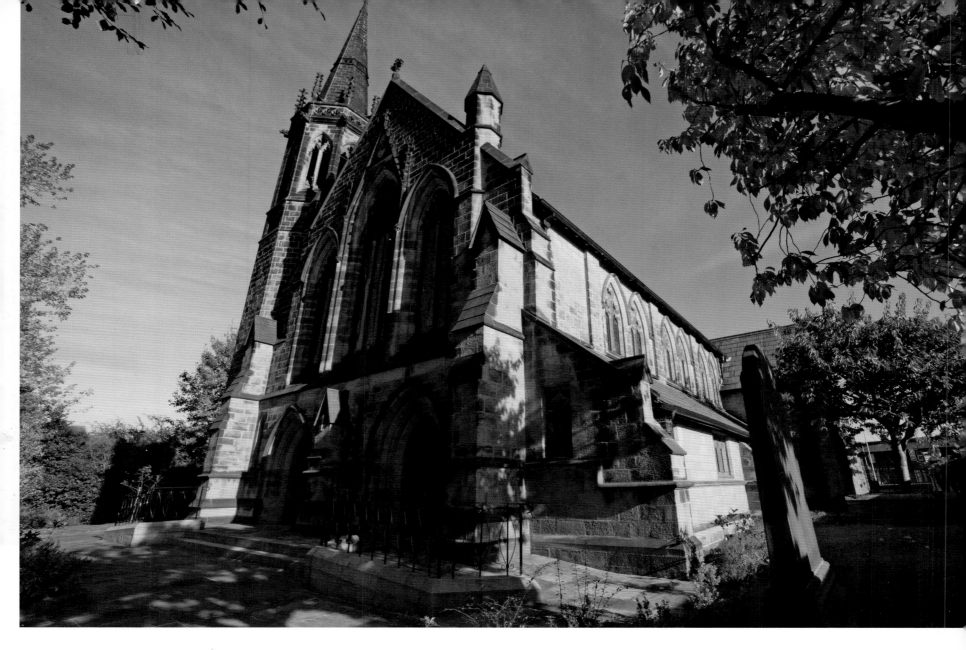

Chippendale

The famous furniture-maker Thomas Chippendale (1718-79) was born at Farnley near Otley and his statue now stands in the town near to the old site of Prince Henry's Grammar School (right) where he was a pupil. Among his many commissions he provided furniture for country houses in Yorkshire including Harewood House, Nostell Priory, Temple Newsam and Burton Constable Hall. Like all market towns, Otley has a wide range of public houses and at one point was being considered as the town with more pubs per head of the population than any other!

Harewood House

This magnificent country house, to the north of Leeds, is the home of Earl and Countess Lascelles. It was built by the York architect John Carr between 1759 and 1772 on the instructions of Edwin Lascelles whose father had made his

fortune in the ribbon trade, from his position as collector of customs in Barbados and his directorship of the East India Company. There had been a previous house on the site, Gawthorpe Hall, which was demolished just

before the completion of Harewood House. Over a six year period from 1843 the south facade of the house was remodelled by Sir Charles Barry. He increased the relief of the features on the façade, added balconies to

Immediately beyond the house to the south is a large and elaborate Italianate parterre with intricately-shaped flower beds, fountains and herbaceous borders. When viewed from the raised terrace in front of the house or from an upstairs window the effect is dazzling. A scalloped pool lies at the centre of the parterre with a statue of Orpheus standing in the middle. On either side are star-shaped pools with Tritons (half human and half dolphin) spouting water. The flower beds, which are full of spring and summer bedding according to season, are box-hedged, with urns and clipped yews in the shape of cones. The grounds of the house were landscaped by Lancelot "Capability" Brown between 1758 and 1774. He dammed Gawthorpe Beck to create a serpentine lake and planted groups of trees on the slopes on either side of the lake. The whole landscaped park is idyllic and it is hard to believe that it is not perfectly natural.

some of the windows, and built a roof balustrade and a large outdoor staircase. The interiors were the work of Robert Adam and much of the furniture is documented work by Thomas Chippendale. John Carr also designed the estate village of Harewood.

Wetherby

The attractive market town of Wetherby lies in the extreme north-east corner of Leeds Metropolitan District. It is located at an important bridging point on the north bank of the river Wharfe where the river was crossed by the Great North Road, the A1, which now bypasses the town. The town has had a market charter since 1240. The charter granted to the then landowners, the Knights Templar, a Thursday market and a three-day annual fair. In the early 17th century the Cavendish family (the Dukes of Devonshire) became the main landowners but they sold their landed interests in the town in a great sale in 1824. The town is now partly a commuter town for York, Leeds and Harrogate. It is also well-known for its racecourse. The present Wetherby racecourse, which opened in 1891 on York Road, is unusual in that it does not hold flat races but only jump races.

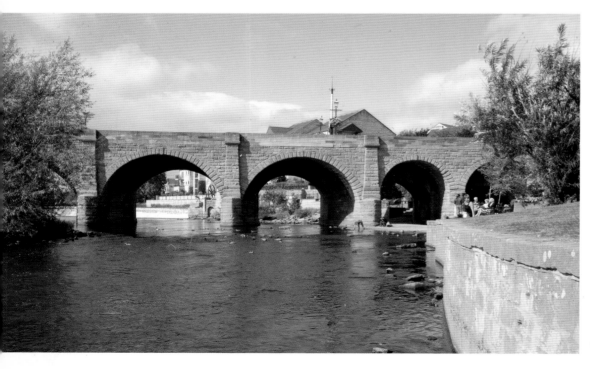

Besides the bridge, with two of its six arches considered to be medieval, the town contains a small town hall (left) built in 1845 in the Classical style. Being an important market town and coach stop on an important national highway, the town was once full of inns. There are now 11 public houses in the town centre including the former coaching inns The Angel (below) and the Swan and Talbot (bottom right) both originating in the 18th century.

Aberford

The small village of
Aberford lies eight miles
to the east of Leeds city
centre. It is home to
some interesting
buildings and
monuments, the most
remarkable of which
are the Gascoigne
almshouses (right).
These date from 1844
and are built in the
Gothic style with many
gables, pinnacles and a
magnificent central
tower. The architect,
George Fowler Jones,
was only 26 when he
designed the alms-
houses. They were
intended to house eight
elderly tenants of the
Gascoigne estate.
Just to the west of
Aberford, is a most
unusual monument
(below). This is a stone
triumphal arch with three
arches, two small ones
on either side and a large
one in the middle. It was
erected in 1783 by
Sir Thomas Gascoigne

who lived at nearby
Parlington Hall (largely
demolished more than 50
years ago).
It is unusual in that it
celebrates the American
victory in the War of
Independence. In fine
lettering at the top of the
monument it states
"Liberty in N America
Triumphant".
Aberford's church,
St Ricarius, has some
interesting features.
Although largely Victorian
(built in 1861) it contains
surviving features from a
much earlier Norman
church.

Boston Spa

Boston Spa, 12 miles north-east of Leeds beside the river Wharfe, became a spa in 1744. Then and into the 19th century it was called Thorp Spa. The central part of the High Street (left and above) is the commercial heart of Boston, but there are also some surviving Georgian houses along the street built by rich merchants from neighbouring towns wishing to spend part of the year at the spa. Now it is a large commuter village (population 4,500) for Leeds, Harrogate and York but is probably best known as the location of part of the British Library, housing more than 7million volumes.

121

Oulton Hall

Oulton Hall (left and above), five miles south-east of Leeds city centre, was built in 1851 to replace an earlier hall destroyed by fire. It is two-storeyed and built in stone in the Classical style with interesting tripartite windows. It has now been converted into a luxury hotel and the surrounding parkland is a golf course. At the park gates stands a half-timbered house (right), with an extension of 1611 dated in an inscription on its gable. The house is a rarity in West Yorkshire where, for the last 400 years, stone and brick have been the main building materials. It is typical of the timber framing in the north of England, in that the external timbers are closely set. This is called "close studding".

Ledston Hall

This grand house, built of Magnesian Limestone, appears at first sight to be of one build in the mid-17th century but in fact is the result of a number of re-builds and extensions. The site of the house was once a grange for the monks of Pontefract Priory and the undercroft of their early 13th century chapel still survives as part of the building. The east front (above) with its projecting wings, Dutch-looking gables and turrets capped by domes was probably built on behalf of Sir John Lewis, a rich East India merchant who bought the house in 1653.

Ledsham

The small village of Ledsham lies 10 miles to the east of Leeds city centre. One of the gems in the village is St John's Hospital, a row of 11 almshouses in Magnesian Limestone built in 1670 by Sir John Lewis, squire of the neighbouring Ledston Hall. But dominating the village is All Saints church. This is basically a Saxon church with later additions. The tower was originally a Saxon porch, heightened in the Norman period and then surmounted by a Perpendicular spire. The "Saxon" doorway in the tower is in fact part of an 1871 restoration.

Local benefactors

Inside the church there are three very interesting monuments to local benefactors. First there is a monument to Sir John and Lady Lewis dating from 1677. Both figures are semi-reclining, resting on an elbow. Another is of Lady Mary Bolles who died in 1662. She lies in a white marble shroud on a tombchest of black and white marble. The third monument is to Lady Elizabeth Hastings, granddaughter of Sir John Lewis who died in 1739. Like her grandfather she rests on an elbow, this time reading. To the left and right of her are life-size figures of her two step-sisters.

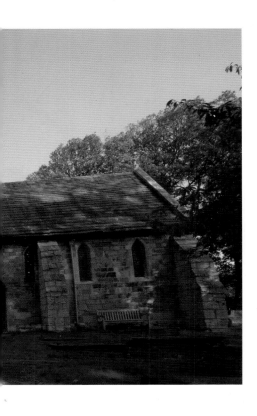

Fulneck

Fulneck, named after a Moravian village in the Czech Republic, was established in 1744 by members of a Protestant episcopal church that had its origins in Bohemia. In 1743 Benjamin Ingham, a Church of England minister, bought the 22-acre Fulneck estate in Pudsey, north-west of Leeds and leased it to the Moravians so that they could set up a Yorkshire colony. They attracted converts from West Riding weavers and set up an industrial village and religious community. The community was governed by a strict moral code, the workers getting a regular wage for their work but with all profits going to the community.

The Moravian settlement is almost entirely in the form of one long row of buildings, called The Terrace (above and bottom left) which was begun in the 1740s as separate buildings but which became almost one continuous line of buildings by the early 19th century. At the centre of the terrace is Grace Hall, which incorporated the chapel, houses for two ministers and school accommodation. At either end of The Terrace are identical houses (far left) for the single men (Brethren) and single women (Sisters). Famous people who have attended Fulneck Shool include James Montgomery, poet and hymn writer (*Angels from the Realms of Glory*), Herbert Asquith, Prime Minister from 1908-16, and Diana Rigg, the actress.